L is for

LONDON

Harriet Rowe

A is for Arches

For 500 years, prisoners would 'go west' to the Tyburn Tree (near Marble Arch) to be hanged in front of crowds large enough to fill Wembley.

Hello, 'ello, 'ello ... Bobbies are named after Sir Robert Peel, who created the first police force in 1829. If you get lost in London, ask a policeman.

Hickory dickory dock, a flock of starlings stopped the clock. They landed on the minute hand of Big Ben in 1945 and moved it back by five minutes.

B is for Bobby

C is for Cathedrals

Saint Paul's is the fifth Cathedral on the site. The previous one had the tallest ever spire and burned down in the Great Fire of London.

That's just not cricket! A cricket ball killed a sparrow in 1936. The bird now perches in the museum at Lords - the 'Home of Cricket'.

BUS STOP
Saint Paul's Cathedral

| 31 | 47 |
| 58 | N21 |

D is for Double Deckers

All aboard! Catch a ride on a double decker but don't get caught at the London Dungeon.

Read all about it! Eros in Piccadilly Circus commemorates Lord Shaftesbury and can be seen on the front page of London's evening newspaper.

E

is for Eros

F is for Fire

The Great Fire of London of 1666 started in a baker's shop in Pudding Lane. It destroyed 89 churches, 400 streets, but only six people died.

The Monument is the tallest free-standing stone column and commemorates the Great Fire. The copper urn on top represents the flames.

G is for Greenwich Meridian

'North, south, east, west - London is best.' Stand on the Meridian Line with one foot in the eastern hemisphere and one in the west.

H

is for

Horse Guards

I

is for Inns of Court

Squiffy Your Honour? Lawyers at Lincoln's Inn sit while toasting guests to commemorate a visit by King Charles II when everyone was too drunk to stand up.

J is for Jellied eels

Jellied eels are enjoyed by Pearly Kings in London's East End. King Henry I wouldn't have been so keen. He died in 1135 after eating an eel.

Off with their heads! Henry VIII played tennis at Hampton Court Palace while his wife, Anne Boleyn, lost her head at the Tower of London.

is for **Kings**

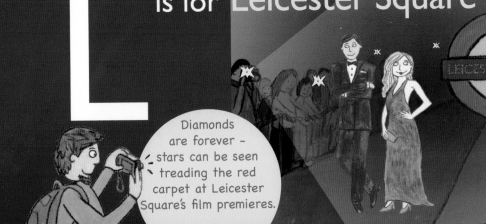

is for Leicester Square

Diamonds are forever - stars can be seen treading the red carpet at Leicester Square's film premieres.

M is for Museums

London has hundreds of museums. You can see everything from the oldest Egyptian mummy to a space capsule that circled the moon.

N

is for

Nelson's Column

Lord Nelson joined the Royal Navy as a boy and lost an eye and an arm in battle. He led Britain to victory at the Battle of Trafalgar but died in the fight.

O

is for

Opera House

Watch the Changing of the Guard at Buckingham Palace. The flag flying on top is the Royal Standard and shows that the monarch is at home.

P

is for

Palaces

Queen Victoria appeared on the first ever stamp in 1840. British stamps are still identified by an image of the monarch - not by country name.

Q

is for

Queen

R is for River Thames

Mind the Gap! In 1952, a number 78 bus jumped the gap after Tower Bridge started to lift its deck to allow a boat to pass underneath.

Detective Sherlock Holmes lived at 221b Baker Street.

S

is for Shopping

In 1909, two men raced a marathon over 524 circuits of the Royal Albert Hall – one finished. A century later 35,000 people ran the London Marathon.

T is for Theatres

London taxis are all registered as Hackney (or horsedrawn) Carriages. The taximeter used to calculate fares gives taxis their name.

The world's oldest underground railway was opened in 1863 and is known as the Tube. Around 80,000 umbrellas are lost each year on the trains.

U is for

Cleopatra's Needle is more than 3,000 years old. It was a gift from the Egyptian ruler, but nearly sank on its voyage to London in 1877.

V is for Victoria Embankment

Wimbledon

W is for

Anyone for tennis? Since its launch in 1877, the tennis tournament on the lawns of south west London remains the largest in the world.

X is for oXo Tower

Don't forget the gravy! The OXO Tower was once a meat factory and now houses shops and restaurants.

Y is for Yeoman Warder

Yeoman Warders, or Beefeaters, guard the Tower and look after the ravens. The monarchy and Tower will crumble if the ravens ever leave.

King John kept lions and bears at the Tower of London in 1204. The animals were finally moved to London Zoo in 1831.

London Zoo was the first scientific Zoo. It was founded by Sir Stamford Raffles, who is better known for founding Singapore (the Lion City).

Z is for Zoo

L is for London

Find out more fascinating facts about
London at
www.hogsbackbooks.com

Coming soon - other books in our
A is for Alphabet
series.

Hogs Back Books - a nose for a good book

A a – Arches
B b – Bobby
C c – Cathedrals
D d – Double Deckers
E e – Eros
F f – Fire
G g – Greenwich Meridian
H h – Horse Guards Parade

I i – Inns of Court
J j – Jellied Eels
K k – Kings
L l – Leicester Square
M m – Museums
N n – Nelson's Column
O o – Opera House

The Gherkin

Saint Paul's
Cathedral

Tower Bridge

London is the capital of the United Kingdom and the biggest city in Europe. There is so much to see and do and you'll always spot a pigeon.

Published
by Hogs Back
Books Ltd, The Stables,
Down Place, Hogs Back,
Guildford, GU3 1DE.
Copyright Hogs Back Books
2011. Illustrations copyright
Harriet Rowe 2011.
Printed in China.
ISBN 9781907432088

For Caron